Monster Trucks
on the Go

by Kerry Dinmont

BUMBA BooKS™

LERNER PUBLICATIONS ◆ MINNEAPOLIS

Note to Educators:

Throughout this book, you'll find critical thinking questions. These can be used to engage young readers in thinking critically about the topic and in using the text and photos to do so.

Lerner Publications Company
A division of Lerner Publishing Group, Inc.
241 First Avenue North
Minneapolis, MN 55401 USA

For reading levels and more information, look up this title at www.lernerbooks.com.

Library of Congress Cataloging-in-Publication Data

The Cataloging-in-Publication Data for Monster Trucks on the Go is on file at the Library of Congress.
ISBN 978-1-5124-1445-5 (lib. bdg.)
ISBN 978-1-5124-1481-3 (pbk.)
ISBN 978-1-5124-1482-0 (EB pdf)

Manufactured in the United States of America
1 – VP – 7/15/16

LERNER
SOURCE

Expand learning beyond the printed book. Download free, complementary educational resources for this book from our website, www.lerneresource.com.

Table of Contents

Monster Trucks

Monster trucks are very large

pickup trucks.

People watch monster truck shows.

Why do you think they are called monster trucks?

Monster trucks are heavy.

They are tall.

Each one is taller than

a person.

Men and women drive
monster trucks.
People can meet the
drivers and see the trucks
before the show.

Most shows are in stadiums.

The stadiums are filled with dirt

jumps and tracks.

Monster trucks are painted.

Some look like animals.

Others have flames or teeth painted on them.

Why do you think people paint monster trucks?

Monster trucks have four big tires.

They can drive on one wheel.

Monster trucks do tricks.

They can climb over almost
anything.

They crush cars.

How do you
think monster
trucks can climb
over cars?

Two trucks race.

The first to cross the finish line wins!

Monster truck shows

are loud.

They are fun to watch.

Do you want to see

a show?

Parts of a Monster Truck

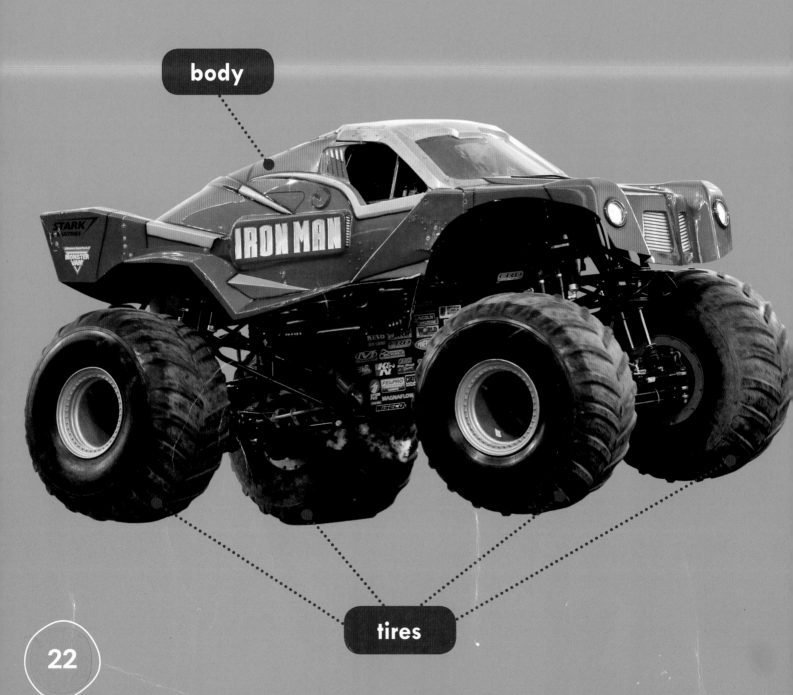

body

tires

Picture Glossary

jumps

bumps or hills
on the track

painted

covered in paint

stadiums

large structures where
events are held

tricks

skills done to
entertain

23

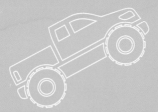

Index

Read More

Bach, Rachel. *The Monster Truck Race.* Mankato, MN: Amicus, 2017.

Gordon, Nick. *Monster Trucks.* Minneapolis: Bellwether Media, 2014.

Silverman, Buffy. *How Do Monster Trucks Work?* Minneapolis: Lerner Publications, 2016.

Photo Credits

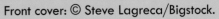